Room *for* Children

Room *for* Children

Stylish Spaces *for* Sleep and Play

Susanna Salk

RIZZOLI
NEW YORK

New York · Paris · London · Milan

FOREWORD
by Kelly Wearstler

page **7**

INTRODUCTION

page **12**

The
Nursery

page **20**

Kids'
ROOMS
page **48**

Work *and* Play
AREAS
page **176**

DESIGNER *and*
PHOTOGRAPHY CREDITS
236

ACKNOWLEDGMENTS
239

FOREWORD

The most important thing in children's room design is to involve the kids early in the process. I always advise parents to let their children pick the colors of their bedrooms, even the concept. The room could have one big idea or just be simple and colorful. It's essential that children enjoy their space and make it feel like their own. After all, it's the room they spend the most time in.

When designing my sons' rooms, it was important to me to create spaces they could grow into, rather than designing for their ages at that exact moment. As a mother and an interior designer, I wanted their rooms to be spirited and playful, but also functional and practical. They're kids, and they need a place to play, read and hang out with their friends.

I think it's nice to use a mix of vintage and new furniture to give the rooms some soul. And lighting is a key element—I like to install great task lighting for their work or whatever fun they have in mind.

My son Oliver chose blue for his bedroom because it was his favorite color. As he was two at the time, I created a room that had ample space for crawling, games, and reading—and room for him to play with his younger brother, Elliott. I used soft furniture and an upholstered bed so there would be fewer boo-boos! Blackout window treatments helped ensure naptime went smoothly.

When Elliott was a baby, I chose yellow for his room because it's such a happy color. He was sleeping

FOLLOWING PAGES Designer Kelly Wearstler chose blue for her son Oliver's room as it is his favorite color. Since he was graduating from a crib, she designed a smaller bed, encased to create a cozier feeling. Tall cabinets flanking the bed reinforce the high ceilings, but with their contents covered they stay anonymous and the toys don't steal the show.

in a crib but already responded to animals, which led me to select the oversized vintage silkscreen of a horse for his room. The comfy chairs were for my husband and me to sit in while we read to him.

Our nightly ritual involves reading or playing a game with both boys and takes place in Oliver's bedroom, which has a huge window overlooking a favorite tree in our yard. The view is incredible and reminds us of being in a tree house.

I think the proudest moment in my career was when my sons told me how much they loved their rooms.

The children's spaces celebrated in these pages are as creative as they are functional and as inspirational as they are aspirational. They reflect not only the child's personality, but the spirit and love of their family.

—*Kelly Wearstler*

Kelly used lots of yellow when decorating her son's nursery—at the time, she didn't know whether she was having a boy or a girl. It's a small room, so she upholstered the walls in a yellow moire fabric to make it quiet and warm. The painted horse textile is all about the scale and the fantasy of the image. She acquired it from a textile dealer and immediately knew it was the one dramatic piece that would complete the room.

INTRODUCTION

By Susanna Salk

"Whatever you do, just don't make it all white!" So proclaimed my friend and mother of two, Martine, about how I should decorate my soon-to-be-firstborn-son's nursery. This was more than ten years ago. At the time, my choices for boys' decor were Barbar, soldiers, teddy bears and trains. Internet shopping hadn't quite taken hold yet and the retail options—even though I lived in Los Angeles at the time— were pretty slim. I was at the end of my second trimester perusing the same baby store on La Brea Boulevard everyone else did. Inside were rows of barren cribs arranged according to price. Once you got past the guilt of not buying the Italian brand you could not pronounce, you would select your crib and order the bars stained either white or brown. The only opportunity to get creative was in the fabric design of the crib bumpers or with the mobile, which would dangle over your beloved infant's face. (And how daring did one want to get there anyway?)

Overwhelmed, I did the exact opposite of what Martine told me to do: I chose a white crib and white baby bumpers. Wasn't white timelessly serene? And shouldn't the nursery be like a blank canvas with my son the most

ABOVE Uglydolls are Winston's favorite bedtime companions.

RIGHT I was tired of always seeing navy blue when it came to boys' rooms, so I painted the walls of my youngest son's room a serene light violet and the bed and floors all white for a surreal feel. I added the curtains around his bed; he loves to close them and do puppet shows. The magnetic chalkboard is an ideal way to display a rotating gallery of photos and drawings.

colorful object in its center? My husband and I pushed the envelope only in what we decided not to do: we were not going to "invest" in one of those hideous "gliders." I bought a chic lounge chair instead. (And I didn't regret it; months later, as Oliver's little body would finally lay asleep in my arms in the thin light of dawn, the weary motherhood hours seemed a little more glamorous thanks to the curved lines of that chaise). We also nixed buying a changing table. Why spend money on something so function-specific? He was going to be out of diapers in just a matter of months. Of course, toilet training ended up taking longer than that, but we much preferred enduring it via the chic adult bureau we transformed with its simple terry cloth cushion on top.

When we moved two years later from our Los Angeles cottage to an 1800s Colonial in Connecticut, I wanted to have Oliver's new bedroom painted in time for our cross-country arrival, so it would be ready for his now-very-exploratory self. This time, I wanted something more than white. I couldn't stop thinking of a room I had seen in a magazine that had sea glass green on the floors, robin's egg blue for the walls, and the palest sky blue on the ceiling. It looked childlike but sophisticated. Serene enough to sleep in, yet stimulating enough for a rousing round of Chutes and Ladders. I bought a color wheel and, like a mad scientist, spun through hundreds of swatches with such cheerful names as "Go Go Green" trying to find the exact matches to the palettes in the photograph. When I finally chose the closest colors, I dialed a local painter and relayed to him the combination of paint numbers. There was a very long pause. Then he said, "Are you sure?" I wasn't at all, but I gave him the go-ahead. Two weeks later, we arrived East at our rather derelict new home. There were no shades or light bulbs and the bathrooms hadn't been painted since the Carter administration, but there was a promising smell of fresh paint wafting down from the second floor. I ran

Grown-up curtains give this space some needed texture without darkening it. Winston loves the exotic way the Moroccan-style bureau showcases his treasures and I love how it transformed a drab wall. I added a mirror from Target and some lanterns from Chinatown to create instant mood.

upstairs to Oliver's new room. Then I was sure. The blues and greens seemed to glide alongside one another in the afternoon sun like tropical fish. The space already had a kind of shimmering personality to it and my son hadn't even set up shop yet. Eleven years later, the colors remain.

Everything else has changed, as I've hurried to keep abreast of my rapidly growing boy and the many demands of his evolving life: the crib was eventually replaced by bunk beds for sleepovers and a desk was added once nightly homework began. The Thomas the Tank Engine train tracks, nailed into imaginative shapes on a low custom table my husband made (necessity being the mother of invention), eventually gave way to a glorious sprawling Lego city that accommodated Oliver's growing height and imagination. A few years later, the Lego city was demolished one Saturday morning when he suddenly announced he didn't need it anymore. As he tore off the tiny bridges and buildings we had so painstakingly built over the course of many Saturday mornings, I gulped back tears. He was excited for the grown-up change and I had to champion it, even though I felt we were plucking away the last vestiges of his childhood. Within minutes after the Lego bins had been rolled out, a bigger desk and bed, and a surfboard coffee table moved in. A psychedelic poster of Jimi Hendrix now reigned over a newly formed kingdom of electric guitars, textbooks, and unmatched socks.

By the time our second son, Winston, came along, design for children had exploded into a full-blown industry, offering everything from lacquered black cribs to eco-friendly crib sheets printed with Andy Warhol artwork. In fact, you didn't even have to go to a children's section anymore to find furniture for your kids' rooms. Parents were simply taking the pieces they loved and putting them into their kids' bedrooms in new, inventive ways. Glossy shelter magazines were suddenly

I found the Jimi Hendrix poster online for less than ten dollars and it set just the right tone for my electric-guitar-playing teenager. I kept the feeling bold with big patterns for the rug, sheets, and headboard frame and cozy with a small floor sofa. I framed a still life Oliver made in fifth grade and placed it above the bed: I think it's important for kids to be reminded of their childhood through the artwork they create.

featuring hip kids jumping on chic sofas on their covers. Top designers didn't blink when commissioned to help create play areas that would rival most living rooms on the style radar: an eighteenth-century French armoire for a 'tween girl's burgeoning wardrobe; bowling alleys in basements with vintage pinball machines; custom-made space suits for twin boys to wear playing laser tag inside their silver-painted Tribeca loft. Design for children had, for better or worse, arrived.

And whether such indulgence is simply another way parents overcompensate—or, perhaps, under-appreciate the simple power of a cozy bed and an entertaining bedtime story—at the end of the day, if design is done right, it's never just about your child having a Lucite desk for doing his math homework. It's about understanding the importance of helping our children create a private world where they can discover who they are and all they were meant to be. Every room in this book was created for that reason. These are all real rooms with real children living in them. Even if the location, square footage, or decor is beyond your budget, in every instance there are abundant ideas that can be—like a favorite box of candy—shared and savored.

My older son will soon be revising his room yet again to accommodate his passage into high school. When I think back on all the many incarnations this simple space has experienced, I marvel at how it was always the exact reflection of who he was, of what he loved at that moment, and who he wanted to become. It sheltered him, punished him, and embraced him. I'm not sure how his room will evolve as he becomes a young man. But I know it will always be waiting for him. And I hope it will never stop being a place where his imagination can be free.

The desk is actually an old door we found in the basement and painted white. It gives you the luxury of length to spread out and display stuff without making the bedroom feel too "office-y." Since Winston is a Lego fanatic I bought three colored bins for storage and tucked them underneath. The blue dust pan makes for a handy shovel when quick pickups are a necessity.

the Nursery

After the mother's stomach, the nursery is the first visible sign that we, as parents, are literally making room for a baby. The responsibility of creating an external womb is intimidating: should we extend the soothing serenity with lots of white and soft surfaces, and let the baby's immediate needs dictate the layout? Or do we welcome the challenge with as much design flair and fanfare as possible?

We don't know yet whether this little person will have a future penchant for chintz or chartreuse. For the time being, she certainly won't care about her nursery's decor so long as she is being held and loved. But the days of simply plunking down a crib, a rocker, and a diaper pail are over. Thanks to the influx of strong design options for

This nursery has a pared-down feeling to it that is soothing. The clean Scandinavian lines of the wood furniture leave visual room for the bolder touches like the green pear and orange bookcase.

the nursery set, parents are being inspired to look beyond the laundry list of what a good nursery "must" possess and are instead feeling empowered to create spaces that feel as unique as a fingerprint.

Some may say the bells and whistles of good design are wasted on such little eyes and that snazzy nurseries are merely the parents' ego on display. But I say, we deserve to flex our design muscles if so inclined. After all, we are making the sudden sacrifice of converting an entire room (or corner of a room!) for this new family member, so why should our style stop at the nursery door?

Ultimately, a successful nursery is as much about making your baby feel welcomed and comfortable as it is about telling the world how excited you are to have your new family member in it.

Who says a pink floor can't be gutsy? The white shag rug offers the perfect companionship as do the equally bold patterned chair and butterfly shade. As a result, the giraffe looks like it's walking in a jungle of unique color.

Babies can handle a lot
more decor excitement than
we give them credit for! The
green border of the curtain
is picked up in the crib bed.
The graphic daybed beneath
framed artwork ensures
the other side of the room
doesn't disappear and
creates visual space and
excitement.

LEFT Taking care of a newborn requires lots of industrial strength and some prefer that their nursery reflects that no-nonsense sensibility. Here the cement walls are punctuated with colorful miniature dolls whose unexpected presence lifts their stature from ordinary toy to mini-sculpture.

RIGHT Shades of soft gray and a stenciled white forest make for an enchanted and very personal welcome for newborn twins.

BISHOP & FORD

This loft space of a
single mother instantly
transforms into a stylish
nursery thanks to the
help of a white partition
(which then becomes
a gallery of framed
photographs), an elegant
chandelier, and two
cheerful antique chairs.
The mother's bed is on
the other side of the
wall.

LEFT It's easy to make a nursery look like a fairy tale: the key lies in the contrasting yet compatible fabrics, tufted walls, bows, ruffles and magical lighting fixtures. The sheer canopy over the bed and the whimsical window treatment complete the feeling.

ABOVE This nursery was designed for boy and girl twins. The alphabet letters reflect a "build them for learning" philosophy. The cribs were dado-wainscotted in car paint and an empire chest has become a changing table. The floorboard stripes have a whimsical feel.

31

Four boys share this one space: the youngest two sleep in facing cribs with the bigger boys' beds nearby. The large room has its specific sleep, play, and study areas. As they do for the rest of the house, the parents let contemporary art be the focal point here.

34 ABOVE The parents wanted a bright nursery that emulated the colors of Morocco. The designer found five Moroccan lanterns covered in silk patterns and wired them on a bamboo rod. They set the tone for the fabrics and the bold and colorful patterns on the bumper and pillows.

RIGHT This nursery's exotic components are grounded by the dark shape of the crib and daybeds and are softened by the white shag rug. The paper lanterns are a unique mobile and the floral border breaks up a white wall while maintaining its Zen-like qualities.

Photographer Pieter
Estersohn created digital
canvas walls for his son's
room from a photo of
his own bedroom when
he lived at the Maharani
of Deogarh's palace,
outside Udaipur in India.
"I wanted an image that
had some depth, as the
room was small," he says.
The richly patterned rug
belonged to Estersohn as
a boy.

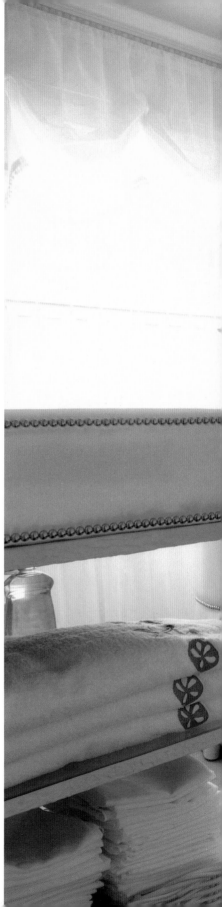

ABOVE The room's practical elements look as chic as the artistic ones thanks to their crisp white lines.

RIGHT A nursery can be as sophisticated as it is soothing. A crib with white patent leather and satin trim looks as sleek and sturdy as an ocean liner, while the boldly patterned chair anchors the room's ethereal elements.

In creating this room,
a soft green seemed
like a safe bet since
the parents didn't know
if they were having a
boy or a girl. A custom
fabric surrounds the
bed, which is crowned
by the alphabet. The
two closets have glazed
doors making the room
feel lighter and the
space more open.

The purple-black wall and
bureau of the same color
add drama and dimension
while still being soothing
enough for a lullaby.
Adding lemon yellow
stripes on the ceiling and
a dash of the same color
inside the all-white crib
furthers the mellow but
cheerful mood.

THIS PAGE This family firmly believes that a child's room should never have second-rate furniture. Case in point: the Herman Miller dresser with snappy hardware blends in beautifully with the childlike environment while still being a design standout.

RIGHT This boy's room is a combination of a few of his mother's personal favorites: stripes and the color turquoise. The old wicker rocker inherited from her grandmother has been re-covered with crisp, tailored fabrics that feel fresh and modern. The back of the Colonial beadboard bookcase echoes the apple green of the rug.

44

BAKER

B

Baker

LEFT When creating a room for her own son, designer Celerie Kemble chose to combine the slick green of the walls with the plush dark blue of the rug. The sides of the crib match the wall, while the white acts as a kind of border between the two intense colors.

RIGHT Bold colors and jungle graphics that seem to grow on the wall echo a child's busy imagination and allow the nursery to remain uncluttered while still feeling full of life.

Kids' ROOMS

It's not just where your child lays his head to sleep at night or does his homework during the day. It's not just a place to play Legos or Green Day, or sip pretend tea or take time-outs. It's his private kingdom. No matter how large or small, shared with siblings or not, it is the one place in the house where your child's dreams are meant to be savored. It is also the space your children will remember for the rest of their lives as first defining them, reflecting who they were and who they were becoming.

Parents have more decorating options than ever before. We can set the stage with every conceivable combination of paint, pattern, and icon. The bedrooms in this chapter—whether decorated with antiques or flea-market finds, modern art on the walls or maps of the world—represent more

This nook is as cozy as it is elegant, thanks to the layers of vibrant, feminine hues and fabrics. The space is further defined by the bamboo trellis tacked neatly along the back wall. It's not all sleep and play here, though: a desk tucked off to the side with its stylish chair proves equally inviting.

than high style for the child. They represent parents' devotion to celebrating that particular stage in their children's lives.

But as much as we become attached to the design we've created for our child, allowing a bedroom to morph and grow along with its occupant is a necessity. As soon as your child progresses from the nursery, his life begins to dictate a redesign, and it's not long before the role of the parents changes from decorator to bystander.

I'll never forget a moment when I was picking up my five-year-old son Oliver from a playdate and I happened upon the bedroom of the friend's teenage brother. I saw Jim Morrison and Britney Spears posters, a mini-fridge, shag carpeting, black walls. The few lights were covered with scarves, and the space gave off a mesmerizing glow. Oliver's small hand grasped mine. "Cool," he whispered in awe. The mother appeared. "Wow," I stammered. "Black walls!" She said she had finally, after many requests, given her son the choice to repaint his room in whatever color he chose. She watched as he excitedly came back from the hardware store and swathed the white walls with a glossy sheen of darkness. I told her I admired her open-mindedness. She shrugged, unwilling to take the credit. "It's him, after all. Him now."

I squeezed Oliver's hand knowing my time to understand would one day come. "Besides, she smiled. "It's only paint."

Painting shelves two different but compatible colors is an easy way to transform a wall. Positioning them next to the curtain and above the bureau creates an instant nook feeling. The garland adds a touch of color and whimsy.

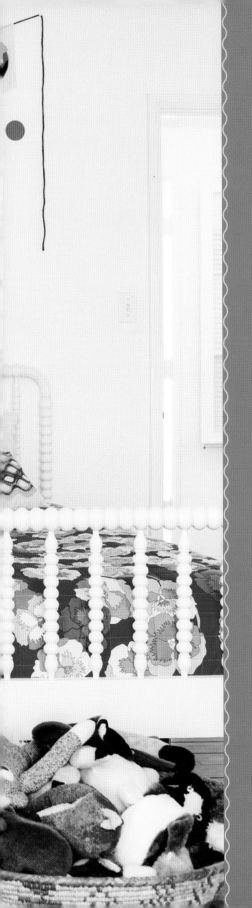

The white walls and beds are the ideal backdrop for a call for peace and play in this shared bedroom. It feels both distinct and unified due to the same color tones used throughout, from mobile to bedspread.

Tangerine is the ideal playmate when it comes to creating a room that is both warm and fun. The kitschy painting above the bed sets the mood, and the furniture follows with its vintage lines.

Oversized polka dots on the floor give a soft room instant depth and mod panache. The colorful posters on the wall augment the mod feeling, and the colorful window shade, bed pillows, and toys tie it all together.

This bedroom solves the problem of siblings with dueling tastes: keep it symmetrical and colorful. The matching sheet sets maintain a lively order, while personal treasures keep identities distinct.

A pink and green combination turns from preppy to playful when the scale is oversized and paired with fanciful yellow animal-patterned wallpaper.

THIS PAGE Sometimes a child's self-portrait is the only decoration you need (not to mention making a unique headboard). The white fabric curtains act as a kind of billowy frame.

RIGHT Try adding soft color for a substantial canopy that doesn't feel too rigid and serves to create drama in a small space.

It's amazing how an
ordinary bed becomes
fit for royal dreams
when fabric is gathered
above the headboard
in traditional European
style. A touch of
modern glamour brings
it up-to-the-minute
thanks to one very red
patterned wall.

BELOW White patent leather walls and a leopard carpet provide a hip juxtaposition to the canopy bed, which is dressed in batiks with hand-embroidered sheets.

RIGHT An investment in one very special piece can make the whole room. This vintage 1963 chair designed by Eero Aarnio has glossy fiberglass on the outside and an upholstered interior that makes for a room within a room.

With its custom-made furniture
this is a child's room that feels
grown-up and will stand the
test of time. A rolling ladder
makes it easy to grab out-of-
reach collectibles, and the
neat compartments of shelves
echo the multi-paned windows.

ABOVE Lots of storage has been added to the upper portion of the room so as not to overcrowd, and a trundle daybed ensures sleepovers happen in the smallest of spaces.

RIGHT As much fun as possible was put into this boy's bedroom nook. The daybed is a great sleeping solution for a small space and the patterned shade ups the whimsy factor.

For designer Amanda Nisbet's fourteen-year-old son, the mandate was to do an orange that felt both palpable and modern. Because the room had to grow with the boy through college, the bed was given an extra tall upholstered headboard with a cutout border applied with nail heads to bring further visual dimension. The tree on the wall is a Curtis Jere sculpture chosen for the organic quality it lends to the room.

If you're going to go with
a theme, go all the way
with style. Here, a cramped
space sets sail, thanks
to a decor that offers
nautical touches from an
oar transformed into a
curtain rod, waves painted
along the floorboards, and
the crisp blue of the boat
bed. The stenciled stars
offer dreamy contemplation
and give a sense of endless
horizon.

LEFT The serenity of the ocean is brought inside with model sailboats hung as art and quiet stripes for pattern. The rug is kept simple so as not to offset the calm factor.

RIGHT This girls' bedroom is at the opposite end of the hall from a noisier boys' bunk room, and coziness and privacy were the goals. The antique chest and painted headboards give a nostalgic sense of serene summers past and present.

This pink and violet bedroom for two young girls is both fun and feminine. The colorful custom starburst carpet combined with the antique "bling" chandelier create a uniquely modern space for the girls to grow in.

Start your child's life adventure early by simply throwing down a faux-leopard carpet and adding British Colonial–style beds draped in khaki and white. Add some oversized friends, and *Out of Africa* becomes out-of-this-world awesome.

THE WORLD
WORLD MAP

Have a child grasp the world's scale from the get-go by using a giant map as wall decor. It beats wallpaper any day. Add wall-to-wall plush carpeting and a tricycle, and you are ready to seize the day.

Old maps accentuate the
distinctive proportions
of this young boy's room,
while the vintage furniture
and toys add an old-world,
fairy-tale feeling. The
safari textile patterns add
to the "world explorer"
atmosphere.

A larger-than-life illustration brings girlish glee to this whimsical room. The bed frames echo the time period of the mural and make you feel like you've stepped into the opened pages of a storybook wearing rose-colored glasses.

The goal was to bring the outdoors in by using a palette of nature's own colors. A mod carpet in blues and greens is paired with the organic-looking fabric of foliage silhouettes on the chair. Custom white lacquer furniture is juxtaposed with bright green walls. A Pop Art quartet in Day-Glow colors provides a strong punctuation point to the natural calm colors of the room.

In this Arts and Crafts house, a child's bedroom features an appliquéd wall hanging depicting the story "Puss 'n Boots." The rest of the room's tones and architectural details all take their cues from these thoughtful, elegant illustrations.

LEFT You don't need fabric or a bunk bed to create a cozy enclosure. This arc of stained wood creates a home within a home for one lucky baseball fan. Painting the ceiling and the walls white keeps the focus on the bed area, where it should be.

RIGHT This classic shingle-style vacation cottage on Cape Cod was all about accommodating a growing family and maximizing the space for visiting friends and family. The lower bunk sleeps two and three other single bunks in the room provide space for a whole family. It's economical and indestructible, yet still elegant.

When stripes work, let them
do all the talking and dial
down the rest of the decor.
Here, the walls give a
space all the personality it
needs and a storage closet
disappears, thanks to some
simple white canvas.

ABOVE White and beige stripes accent the unique height of this bedroom while the dark tones of the four-poster bed keeps things grounded.

RIGHT Four children share this bedroom when they visit their family's pied-à-terre in New York City. Inspired by the Orient Express, the designer created a "compartment" for each child, complete with curtains and bookshelves. The Manhattan skyline at dusk is decoratively painted on the back wall of each compartment.

Painting bunk beds silver
to match the wall trim
gives this bedroom instant
glamour. The close-up
black-and-white portrait
of the sisters clipped
to the railing softens
the cool edges, and the
hanging butterflies and
dragonflies lend a feeling
of femininity.

Make the most of grand scale by accentuating height with symmetrical grand bunk beds that are kept open and inviting via ladders and see-through spaces. By making the center into a living space, guests are made to feel even more welcome. Exotic touches like a zebra rug and antler chandelier ensure matters don't get too serious.

LEFT AND RIGHT This sleeping nook is both magnificent and cozy thanks to the combination of industrial-strength grey and shots of cherry red. "I wanted it to be Marie Antoinette meets Gossip Girl," says designer Diane Bergeron of her daughter's room. The old-world elegance of the striped fabric on the custom bed (which spans the entire room) and the chandelier are the perfect foils for the bold lines of the Eames chair and patterned pillows.

LEFT There's enough careful symmetry amidst the bustling pattern and color to keep you feeling grounded. The quirky lines of the matching built-in compartments above the headboards are echoed in the table below, and the picture frames and pottery lining the shelves bring thoughtful order. The wallpaper is hand-painted and matches the designs on the sides of the beds.

RIGHT Pairing unexpected colors and cozy textures brings surprise sophistication to hard-to-manage corners. Instead of juvenile shapes, try choosing furniture with grown-up appeal. It'll make those late nights of rocking much more enjoyable.

LEFT For one lucky girl, multiple patterns and textures help create a resplendent repose area by the bright light of a window. The muraled screen softens and defines the corner.

RIGHT The classic Greek key motif was a jumping-off point for the room of designer Amanda Nisbet's daughter, especially for the carpet. She notes, "a great pattern can hide a multitude of teenage messes." Wanting to keep the room airy, she chose bright white for the walls, infusing color with the lavender window shade and the bed's headboard. The navy blue trim on the bed skirt grounds the lavender, keeping it from becoming too precious. The blue patent leather on the chair is a dynamic and teen-proof material option.

ABOVE AND RIGHT This bedroom in Bali was designed by the occupant herself. It aptly reflects both the natural beauty of the setting (through its open-air structure and by using wood as its primary material) and the colorful spirit of the girl via the curtained, circular bed and the lavish display of personal objects in her dressing area.

This exotic child's room in
a getaway retreat in Kenya
proves that sometimes
the best decor is to let
the location, and its
architecture, speak for
itself.

Choosing a daybed with unique lines, and then further articulating them by draping a crown arch over the top, is an easy way to bring elegant drama—not to mention height—to a girl's room. The Lucite table is a perfect way to provide storage without taking up visual space, and the color pink acts as a mod mix master.

Mod is the perfect vibe for a 'tween-girl's bedroom, especially when paired with sophisticated pinks. Lots of white acts as the ideal backdrop, allowing the surreal details to punctuate elegantly, not overpoweringly.

Designer Ruthie Sommers chose pink for her daughter's bedroom because "it is the happiest color I know." The chandelier was left by the previous owner and found a second home in the nursery and, when no one purchased the cat in Sommers's store, she adopted it. She loves the green of the carpet, which took three months to arrive from Belgium. "It's the perfect eighties combo with the pink; not too ladies' locker room and not too beach cabana."

ABOVE AND RIGHT This barn space for twin girls was made cozy
by filling it with the many things they love, from dolls to
games, and by decorating in red, the perfect color for the
country. Their parents wanted to make it the equivalent of
a dollhouse, a "little barn" of the girls' own where they
could spend quiet time. Extra-large seating and lighting
(above) encourages longer lounging and reading.

Why settle for just pink,
when you can have PINK!—
especially when it's parlayed
into a playful toile on
the walls and paired with
sunny yellows. The cheerful
contrast of the headboards
against the patterned walls
keeps anything from getting
too frilly or too serious.

Designer and architect
Barbara Bestor created
an attic dream room
for her daughters
that feels open but
still has some visual
privacy. She refashioned
iconic Marimekko duvet
covers into curtains
by placing each panel
onto a hospital curtain
track. The result is
Scandinavian style that
feels as inviting as it
does private.

LEFT AND ABOVE This room is fit for a Moroccan princess who has a particular penchant for pink. The bed curtains give an immediate sense of scale and exotic mystery to the room. Grown-up furniture gets fun when it's juxtaposed in such a lively, unexpected mix like the boldly patterned sheets, large bureaus, and a tufted ottoman. The bubble-gum pink lighting fixture with its outer-worldly shape and the red African headdress bring further levity. Vintage fashion illustrations in colorful frames (above) offer symmetry and fancy to this corner nook of the room.

A double-gabled space gives the sense of being a spacious retreat in the treetops. The children's table is customized with a mirrored glass top for art projects and the rug is a 1960s vintage white shag. The striped curtain offers privacy while keeping the space airy, and it plays off the cheerful yellow pendant.

Designers Bob and Cortney Novogratz's daughters share this room, which celebrates the power of flowers with a wall mural of plastic blooms captured under Plexiglas. The canopy bed is from Bali, and Bob says "it takes our daughters to far-away places."

This elegant alcove was designed for an aspiring ballet dancer. Its mature architecture and furniture will grow with her as she blossoms into a prima ballerina.

Spacious bunk beds in this ski house can feel more like snow palaces, due to the unexpected height of the ceilings and the cool white of the wood. Curtains of Swiss linen can be drawn for privacy or just fun and games.

ABOVE Placing the beds against the walls in this girls' room forms a midcentury corner unit, and drawers under the mattresses add much-needed storage in a tight space. The walls are papered in a small yellow print punctuated by bold art, creating a very happy environment.

RIGHT Orange, white, and blue are perfect playmates in this cheerful and stylish girl's room.

By sticking with one continuous pattern of green and white, the toile almost becomes a neutral and gives this child's room a heightened sense of luxury and comfort.

ABOVE A daybed is the ideal solution for rooms that need to function both as sleeping and living quarters but don't have the luxury of space.

RIGHT This pattern proves that plaid can be both boyish and sophisticated, especially when paired against dark walls. It will also feel relevant as the occupant gets older.

LEFT A spacious, bright room can handle lots of ornamentation, and here every inch delivers with whimsical details that are the stuff of a little girl's dreams.

RIGHT Beams, walls, and a bed draped in creamy white are the perfect backdrop for dreaming.

141

LEFT Like a Mondrian painting come to life, this room dares to make oversized statements in clean, fresh colors. The result is a playful moment that delivers clever storage to boot.

RIGHT This room was created for the children of Miami-based art and design collectors. They wanted to have fun with color and shapes, making a modernist oasis for their kids.

LEFT A small space is given the most style thanks to the fail-safe pairing of blue and white with bunk beds. Notice how the ladders have been smartly positioned on opposite sides to allow for plenty of climb-into-bed space.

ABOVE Red, white, and blue don't just look great on a flag, they also zing when paired with decor. The results could suit either a boy or girl.

LEFT For small rooms, using different tones of the same color for walls, ceiling, and floor makes for a more unified space.

RIGHT Tight spaces need to be tightly edited. Things are kept simple and graphic for this boy's room, with a childhood icon used as the focal point.

A boy's room gets
patriotic without being
too serious thanks
to whimsical touches
like an antique drum
lighting fixture and an
overscaled framed flag
above the bed, which
feels more like art.

Just because a room is small, it doesn't mean that you can't have fun and layer in some personality. Sometimes the more you do to a small space, the bigger it feels.

FOLLOWING PAGES, LEFT The Mediterranean blue is the perfect backdrop for this Michael Jordan portrait, which was painted in Africa on salvaged wood. The black chair was bought at a tag sale and complements Jordan's dramatic stare.

FOLLOWING PAGES, RIGHT Tomato red and Kurt Cobain's smile make for an unexpected yet altogether cheerful choice for this boy's room. The painting above evokes youth's sunny pleasures. White sheets allow the colors to shine.

SURFING GETS sophisticated when it's paired with vintage touches like bamboo borders and framed tropical prints. The beige and white tones are the perfect backdrop to the surprise ceiling.

———

RIGHT Maximize a boy's hangout space by transforming a window seat into a place to sleep, making the main focus the rest of the room, which is perfect for hanging out with friends.

Simplicity can make the most
elegant of statements,
especially in a girl's summerhouse bedroom. Painting
wood floors and walls creamy
white and then keeping them
bare allows a lone painting
to make a major statement:
it's almost as if she's
inviting you into the room.
The layered look of the beds
and slipcovers adds further
warmth.

LEFT Three little girls share this large bedroom in an Upper East Side townhouse. The designer outfitted the room with standard canopy beds and then made them unique with fabric canopies and feathered peaks. The wall of mirrors is actually a series of doors leading to individual cubbies where the girls can hide their toys and clothes.

BELOW Fairy-tale stenciling above the bed echoes a child's sweetest bedtime dreams. The strong patterned headboard keeps things from getting too amorphous.

This girl's room was originally done when she was nine, but was updated when she turned fifteen and wanted a more sophisticated look. She designed it herself, with the help of a decorator, starting with an English regency screen that she saw in a magazine. From there she added a French Napoleon III bergere chair upholstered in blue silk satin and a French bronze coffee table from the 1940s, along with a fur throw and an elegant Oriental rug. The cool blue of the walls reinforces the quiet formality.

THIS PAGE The unexpected surprise of blue, green, and brown, and the white polka dots, makes for a bedroom that could suit either a boy or a girl. The large space is maximized by smart floor-to-ceiling shelving.

———

RIGHT This room was designed for a sophisticated fifteen-year-old. While she wanted pink, it was kept from looking too cute with shots of fuchsia in bold patterns mixed with crisp navy. The Royère-inspired lighting, custom-painted raffia side tables, and grass cloth walls add to the "mature" aesthetic.

The coral pink chandelier adds just the right amount of sophistication to this girl's sitting area. The vintage watercolors are casually framed and hung at a child's eye level, giving the scale of the space a playful feel.

Headboards and curtains are an ideal way to express our inner style, and sometimes confidence is the common denominator that unifies diverse patterns such as zebra with a cowboy western print. The dark wood floors, pale walls, and textured bedspreads are perfectly linked, helping to make this boys' room a walk on the wild side.

Children's rooms are the ideal places to mix fantasy and humor on a grand scale without losing our perspective—or overspending. Here a tropical beach appears to be outside the circular "windows"—just the right trick for rooms without a view. A vintage daybed with formal lines centers the space, while gnome end tables remind you that at the end of the day, it should all be in good fun.

Having fun at the
ceiling's expense is
an easy way to make
a child's summerhouse
bedroom resonate.

LEFT By hanging a vintage picture low, designer Gen Sohr creates a cozy nook in her stepdaughter's bedroom without having to add curtains or walls. The pink cross was originally white but Sohr spray-painted it pink because "I love the idea of this modern iconic piece turned girlie!" It also adds a whimsical modern element to a 1950s vintage-style bathroom.

RIGHT Make the room feel accessible for young ones by keeping the focus at ground level with uncluttered walls and pint-sized furniture. A blackboard wall is an invaluable way to be ready when inspiration strikes.

This attic bedroom in an 1895 Fire Island beach house belongs to a teenage girl. The room retains the house's original dark wood walls, ceilings, and floors, but it is filled with light, airy, modern pieces for contrast. The tie-dyed bedcover, selected by the young occupant from a catalogue, was the spark that inspired the general direction and spirit of the room.

Work *and* Play AREAS

Giving our children room to play and work is as crucial to their growth as sleep. As our first son grew from a squishy blob we could place wherever we wanted to an active toddler with a mind and legs of his own (not to mention a packed playdate schedule), we knew we had to look beyond the four walls of his bedroom to find additional stomping ground for him and his merry tribe. Since we live in New England, there are too many days where being outside is just not an option. Inside felt limited too: our living room was out, too much furniture and too many sharp corners; the kitchen was spacious with lots of counter space but my boys never were the types to sit and color for long; our basement floor was unfinished and filled with too much gear to justify transforming it into an underground lair. One night while

Touches of whimsy take a grown-up fireplace and turn it into fun. The surreal white of the fireplace set against the dark wall—with its inset painted to match—feels almost like a children's book illustration come to life.

lying in bed pondering our dilemma, my husband had a Eureka moment and suddenly made an emphatic pointing gesture upward.

A month later, we tore open half the ceiling of our 1800s Colonial to expose the expansive but musty attic above. Here was precious space, long ago forgotten. We exposed the hidden beams to give the space character and added new windows to let the light pour in. We added an open stairway connecting it with our bedroom and giving playtime its own official entrance. For once, wall-to-wall carpeting was appealing: we bought yards of the cheapest, most plush material we could find from Home Depot and covered every inch of the floor. I bought small tables and chairs from Ikea and hung some circus rings from the ceiling. My son and his friends were swinging upside down before we had time to step out of the way.

We had painted the walls a fresh white, but there was a crawl space that remained untouched during our renovations. One day I chased an errant ball lodged back there and noticed a faded image in a low corner. It was a painted bouquet of daisies with the inscription, "For Sandra, Love Daddy." Almost fifty years earlier a renowned children's book illustrator had lived in the house with his children and had clearly created a playroom out of similar necessity. After he moved, at least half a dozen owners had traipsed in and out before we arrived; one of them must have boarded up the attic, sealing away its history.

Uncovering the evidence of this previous playroom reminded me that accommodating children's boundless energy and imagination is a task as old as time. What has changed are the boundaries of those accommodations. Remember the days of the "rumpus room"? It was just a glorified basement with a shag carpet, located far enough away from the household's main zone so as not to interfere with "grown-up time." Desks were a reminder that school was just around the corner.

Today, when we seek to contain all the little voices and limbs in one space, we aim to do so with the same thought and care for design and style that we used to reserve for our own home offices and studios. The spaces here illustrate how children can unwind as creatively as they can work. Neither walls nor lack of them need limit us. Whimsy counts more than budget. And when kids feel like hiding? An enchanted miniature cottage to call their very own will do just fine. No extra spot to give kids a reading nook? Make one by plunking down a chic beanbag or two under a floor lamp. Not enough refrigerator space to display the daily work of your young artists? Cover an entire wall with magnetic chalkboard. An entire room devoted just for the art of play? If you have the luxury of space, consider this a necessity. The rooms here will inspire you to have fun creating your child's work or play space.

The exotic stripes of this sofa
cheerfully cohabitate with the
solid pastels of the chair and
ottoman, proving you don't
have to match to make the mix
work. The beige carpet and
corkboard walls help balance
out the color, allowing the
children's art to speak for
itself.

Why buy art when personal
expression has the most
impact—and value—of all?
The fanciful touches here
allow a work place not to
take itself too seriously.
The galvanized drawers are
a great way to keep art
and work staples tucked
away elegantly while still
being close at hand.

By mixing unique vintage pieces like the scorecard clock with the bold colors and graphics of the desk and curtains, this area becomes a timeless space where work and play cohabitate.

Who says a boy and girl can't share a room in style? Blue and pink don't need to be segregated, as proven in this happy bedroom with plenty of space for playtime.

An easy way to rev up
a room is by layering
textures and patterns.
Rather than breaking
up the flow of this
room, the desk adds
personality thanks to
its cool cutout circles.

LEFT Kids' walls merit not only their own artwork but that of adult artists as well. If the budget allows, treating children to art they can appreciate is one of the best gifts you can give them.

RIGHT This truck room gives a nod to the nostalgia of American family road trips of the 1950s. Vintage road-map wallpaper and antique trucks reflect the color palette of the period. The two pipe beds car-painted in black lacquer offset the small plaids of the bedding and upholstery (reminiscent of men's cotton shirts of the era). A wall map encourages travelers to pushpin in their travel souvenirs.

Organization can be whimsical
with boldly patterned fabrics
that create a closet both
decorative and functional
when draped open or shut. The
cherry red totes are placed
within easy reach for young
hands. The grand proportions
of the room can handle such
bold inventiveness, yet at the
same time the space is made
accessible to those it caters
to with small-scale furniture.

This play space doesn't
limit a six-year-old
imagination but rather
encourages it, with ample
places to paint, play the
drums, or display personal
masterpieces via the corkboard wall. It is organized
chaos parents can live
with.

What better way to pass
from the grown-up's to
the children's area than
via walls announcing the
young ones' creativity
and schedules? This
passageway lined with
both chalkboards and
corkboards does the trick.

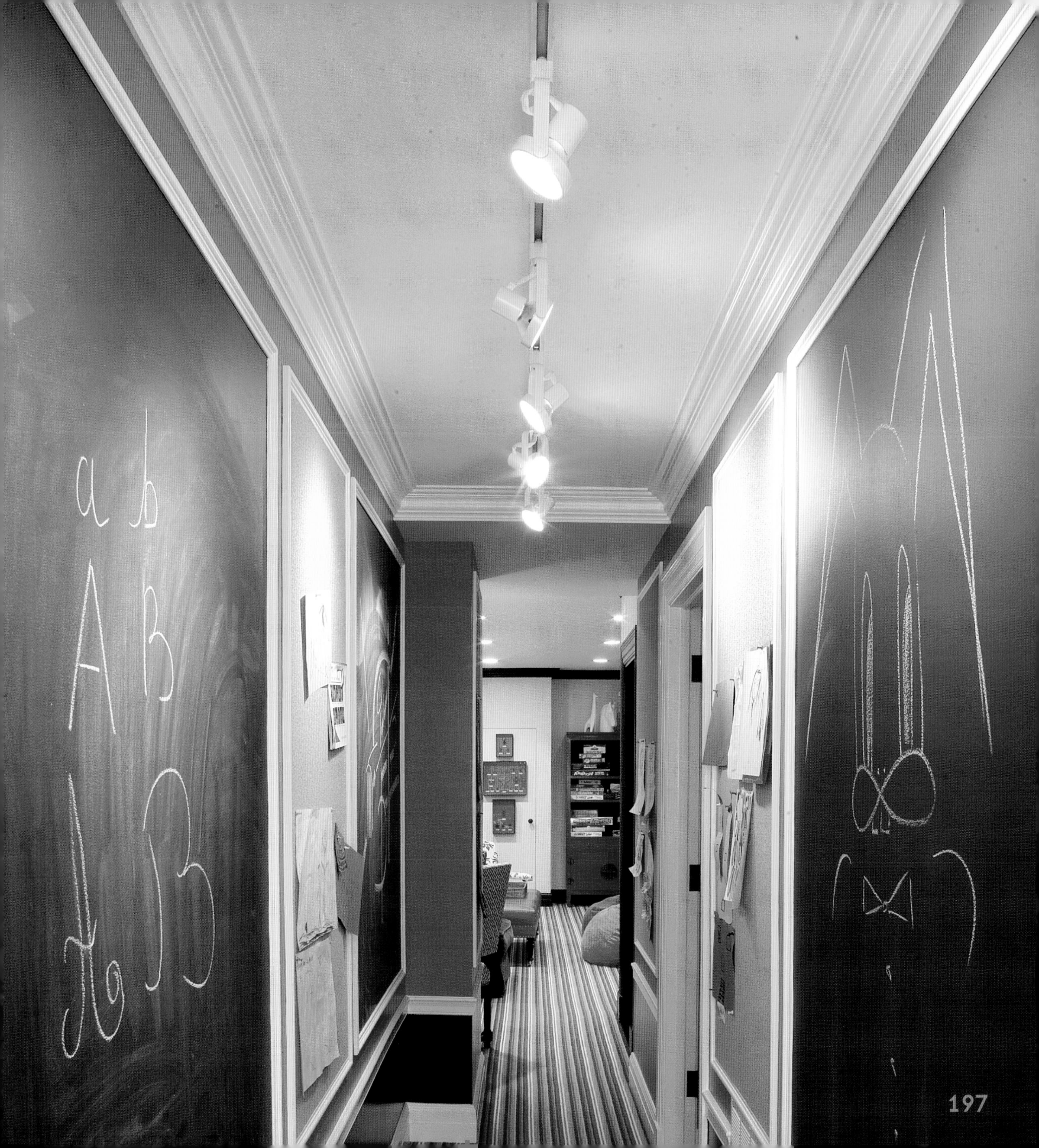

This work area for little scholars has a wonderful utilitarian school-room feel. The table is an enormous old printing table, the legs of which are cut off to accommodate a child's height, and the chairs are from a 1950s-era classroom. Each wall is a different color. The chalkboard green on one wall was chosen to add more depth to the room. The mural was created in the spirit of a family enjoying a sunny day.

If kids have to work, at least surround them with oversized tools of the trade. The festive walls and game wheel make the desk a destination rather than a place to avoid.

White, light, and plenty of space make for an aerie playroom with a view. The sheer window panels shield the outside just enough to keep the focus inward and the whimsical red piping reinforces the unique height of the room.

LEFT Rows of empty shelves and a blank white wall are sometimes all you need in order for children to create. Displaying their creations, framed or unframed, instantly personalizes any corner.

RIGHT Is there such a thing as too much shelving? Not when it comes to helping kids instantly find the book or movie they crave.

The small scale of the
furniture allows for
maximum appreciation of
the architectural details
above. If space allows,
it's nice to give each child
his or her own separate
space to create, complete
with personal storage bin.

LEFT Framed album covers from the 1970s create the ultimate rock tribute on a pure white wall.

RIGHT A hard-to-pin-down white gets grounded thanks to the straight lines of a chocolate desk and shelves. These colors are ideal for a boy who doesn't want the traditional blue or green options.

Designer Eve Robinson created a playroom for her family that is both fun and witty: "I wanted a space my kids could play in from twos to 'tweens that didn't feel juvenile." The cabinet is from an office-furniture supplier and can withstand any gang of five-year-olds. An old biology diagram serves as educational art.

Even if you have the
luxury of space, you don't
need to fill it willy-nilly.
This room has been kept
open for clear thinking,
but an extensive work
station placed along the
wall, with bulletin boards
and shelves above, keeps
the details organized. The
neutral shades of beige
and brown allow kids
to focus, but if a little
procrastination is
in order, building some
Legos is always an option.

A burst of red encourages
you to stop and PLAY.
The smooth floor is ideal
for little wheels, and its
checkerboard pattern
gives a nice texture to
anchor all that color.
The oversized shelves
keep the clutter to a
minimum, and the window
seat is a great way to
accommodate a quick dip
into naptime.

There aren't enough
enchanted spaces in the
world where kids can play
at being grown-up while
still feeling like kids.
Wherever you live and
whatever your space, have
some fun creating one for
your child.

A bike for every
enthusiast, no
matter how small.

LEFT The more fabulous a girl's closet, the more she will want to hang and display her dresses, purses, and tutus. The oversized paisley pattern luxes up an ordinary space, making it worth showing off.

RIGHT It sometimes feels like a locker room with all that kids' stuff around, so why not make it official? These roomy alcoves offer plenty of space to park coats, shoes, even a lacrosse stick. The dark color is sophisticated and unobtrusive enough that the entryway to this summerhouse doesn't feel like a gym.

ABOVE The homey simplicity of a wooden desk and window offers just the right place to display personal crafts and treasures.

RIGHT Sometimes every drawing is worth displaying, especially when put into cheerful colored frames and clustered into happy vignettes.

This child's living space has a unique vintage quality, thanks to antique pieces, sepia tones, and faded blues, greens and yellows, all of which help create a timeless feel.

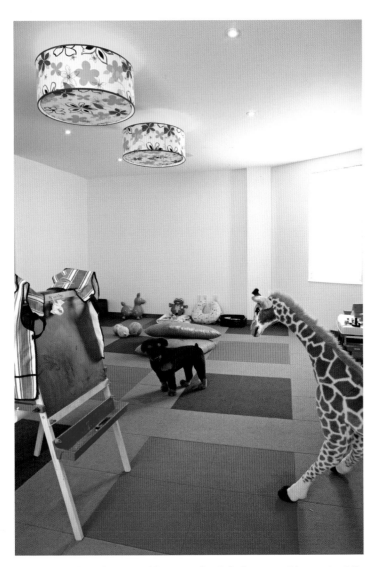

OPPOSITE There's something wonderful about making art while surrounded by framed pieces of prior efforts. This eco-friendly craft room with its large galvanized-metal-topped table and reclaimed metal base encourages the process while honoring the results with the art gallery–like wall. Uniformity is achieved by using simple black frames that dramatically offset the bold black-and-white checked floor.

LEFT Wall-to-wall carpeting is an obvious way to make a space comfortable for little knees and feet, but why not try one with a modern pattern? This one keeps the large space from looking too barren and its masculine squares are offset by the cheerful floral lightshades.

ABOVE If you can afford to do only one thing to transform your child's space, consider a unique wall treatment. This harlequin pattern has staying power due to an overscaled design that feels festive rather than overwhelming.

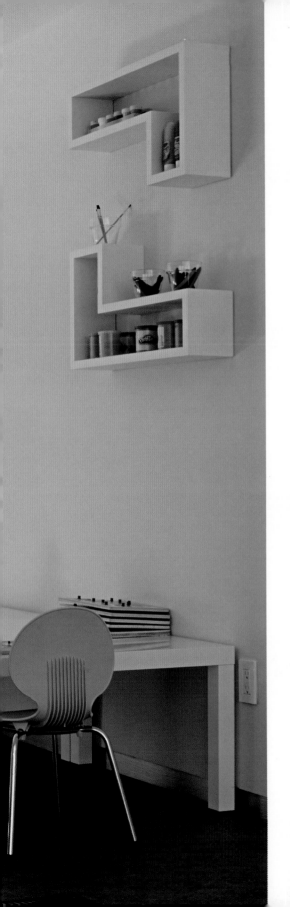

This space is set up to be as functional as a classroom, with a nice long desk area, sturdy chairs and lots of storage space for supplies. It's always nice to add a playful element like a crawl-through tunnel.

Why can't a child's space be glamorous? Painting a cavernous play space a glossy dark color is not only daring but smart: no dirty streaks or crayon marks show up! By taking away furniture and knickknacks (and adding two stupendous lighting pendants, which dangle like earrings) ample room remains for maximum imagination. And by leaving the floor uncarpeted, tricycles can have run of the place.

In urban settings where space is at a premium, one often has to get creative with play spaces. This stainless steel dome built on the roof of a Manhattan building makes for a basketball court with a view.

How to transform a large grown-up room into a kid-friendly space? Insert two large cubbies (painted white to blend in with the walls) and fill them with favorite stuff. A flat-screen television centered above the fireplace further shakes up the formal space. Sprinkle with kids' art and two cool chairs and you're ready to entertain a variety of ages.

DESIGNER CREDITS

FOREWORD
Kelly Wearstler

THE NURSERY
PAGE 24
Jennifer DeLonge

PAGE 27
Selina van der Geest

Page 29
Kim Zimmerman

PAGE 30
Carrido-Young Design

PAGE 31
Windsor Smith

PAGE 33
Sixx Design

PAGE 34
Leslie L. Hunt

Page 36
Pieter Estersohn

Pages 38 & 39
Jamie Drake

Page 41
Charlotte Moss

Page 43
Jenna Lyons

Page 45
Susan Bednar Long

Page 46
Celerie Kemble

KIDS' ROOMS
Page 49
Allison Tick

Pages 54 & 55
Maxine Greenspan

Page 56
Suzanne Sharp for The Rug Company

Page 61
Jonathan Adler

Pages 66 & 67
Alex Papachristidis

Pages 68 & 69
Mark Zeff

Page 70
Katie Ridder

Page 71
Katie Ridder

Page 73
Amanda Nisbet

Page 76
Steven Gambrel of S.R. Gambrel Inc.

Page 77
Orrick and Company

Page 79
Eve Robinson

Pages 88 & 89
Alex Papachristidis

Page 93
Orrick and Company

Page 97
Eve Robinson

Page 100
Platt Byard Dovell White Architects; Tracy Bross design

Pages 102 & 103
Diane Bergeron

Page 106
Richard Holley

Page 107
Amanda Nisbet

Page 112
Sally Markham

Page 115
Sharon Simonaire

Page 116
Ruthie Sommers

Page 121
Philip Gorrivan

Page 122
Barbara Bestor Architecture

Page 124
Barry Dixon

Page 125
Barry Dixon

Page 126 & 127
Barbara Bestor Architecture

Page 128
Sixx Design

Page 131
Maureen Footer

Page 132
Alan Tanksley, Inc.

Page 134
Diamond Baratta Design

Page 135
Judy Nyquist

Page 136
Alessandra Branca

Page 138
Alessandra Branca

Page 139
Alessandra Branca

Page 140
Barry Dixon

Page 142 & 143
Amy Lau Design

Pages 146 & 147
Shaun Jackson Inc.

Page 149
Steven Gambrel of S.R. Gambrel Inc.

Page 152 & 153
Sixx Design

Page 155
Robert Stilin

Page 157
Ellen O'Neill

Page 158
Thomas Jayne

Page 161
Jan Showers

Page 162
Sally Markham

Page 163
Christina Sullivan and Susan Bednar Long of TOCAR

Page 164
Elizabeth Martin Design

Page 172
Genifer Goodman Sohr

Page 174
Thomas Jayne

PLAY AND WORK AREAS
Page 177
Jenna Lyons

Page 181
Eve Robinson

Page 183
Laurence Kriegle

Page 185
Sixx Design

Page 191
Windsor Smith

Page 197
Alessandra Branca

Pages 198 & 199
Elizabeth Martin Design

Page 200
Barry Dixon

Page 203
Alessandra Branca

Pages 206 & 207
Elizabeth Arnold

Page 208
Robert Stilin

Page 209
David Hertz

Page 210
Eve Robinson

Page 217
Thomas Callaway

Page 218
Sixx Design

Page 220
Lisa Pope Westerman

Page 225
Kishani Perera Inc

Page 226
Jillian Pritchard Cooke

Page 228
Lisa Pope Westerman

Page 233
Sixx Design

PHOTOGRAPHER
CREDITS

FOREWORD
Grey Crawford

INTRODUCTION
Page 12
David Prince

Pages 13-18
John Gruen

THE NURSERY
PAGE 21
© Matthew Hranek /
Art + Commerce

PAGE 23
Max Kim-Bee

PAGE 24
Roger Davies

PAGE 26
Costa Picadas

PAGE 27
John Gruen

PAGE 29
Pieter Estersohn

PAGE 30
Photo: Tim Street-Porter

PAGE 31
Cindy Gold

PAGE 33
Joshua McHugh

PAGE 34
Miguel Flores-Vianna

Page 35
© Matthew Hranek / Art +
Commerce

Page 36
Pieter Estersohn

Pages 38 & 39
Edward North

Page 41
Pieter Estersohn

Page 43
Melanie Acevedo

Page 44
Melanie Acevedo

Page 45
John Gruen

Page 46
Zach DeSart

Page 47
Justin Bernhaut

KIDS' ROOMS
Page 49
Melanie Acevedo

Page 51
Melanie Acevedo

Page 52
Max Kim-Bee

Page 55
Tim Street-Porter

Page 56
The Rug Company

Pages 58 & 59
John Gruen
Page 61

Tim Street-Porter

Page 62
Tim Street-Porter

Page 63
Tim Street-Porter

Page 65
Costa Picadas

Pages 66 & 67
John Gruen

Pages 68 & 69
Zeff Design

Page 70
Lucas Allen

Page 71
Scott Frances

Page 73
Tory Williams

Page 74
Tri Giovan

Page 76
© William Abranowicz /
Art + Commerce

Page 77
John Gruen

Page 79
Scott Frances

Pages 80 & 81
Pieter Estersohn

Page 82
Pieter Estersohn

Page 85
Pieter Estersohn

Page 86
Pieter Estersohn

Pages 88 & 89
John Gruen

Pages 90 & 91
Sarah Maingot

Page 92
Tim Street-Porter

Page 93
John Gruen

Page 95
Costa Picadas

Page 96
Tim Street-Porter

Page 97
Peter Margonelli

Page 99
Melanie Acevedo

Page 100
Jonathan Wallen

Pages 102 & 103
Peter Throsby

Page 104
Costa Picadas

Page 105
Costa Picadas

Page 106
Tria Giovan

Page 107
Tory Williams

Page 108
Pieter Estersohn

Page 109
Pieter Estersohn

Page 111
Pieter Estersohn

Page 112
Pieter Estersohn

Page 115
Simon Upton

Page 116
Annie Schlechter

Pages 118 & 119
John Gruen

Page 121
Pieter Estersohn

Page 122
Ray Kachatorian

Page 124
Gordon Beall

Page 125
Gordon Beall

Page 126 & 127
Bruce Hemming

Page 128
Joshua McHugh

Page 131
Daniel Eifert

Page 132
© William Abranowicz /
Art + Commerce

Page 134
Tria Giovan

Page 135
Tria Giovan

Page 136
Thibault Jeanson

Page 138
Thibault Jeanson

Page 139
Thibault Jeanson

Page 140
Tria Giovan

Page 141
Miki Duisterhof

Page 142 & 143
Kris Tamburello

Page 144
Costa Picadas

Page 145
Costa Picadas

Page 149
© William Abranowicz /
Art + Commerce

Page 150
Costa Picadas

Page 152
Costa Picadas

Page 153
Costa Picadas

Page 154
Pieter Estersohn

Page 155
Joshua McHugh

Page 157
Pieter Estersohn

Page 158
William Waldron

Page 159
Costa Picadas

Page 161
Bill Bolin

Page 162
Pieter Estersohn

Page 164
© William Abranowicz /
Art + Commerce

Page: 167
Paul Costello

Page 169
Costa Picadas

Page 171
Costa Picadas

Page 172
Melanie Acevedo

Page 173
Costa Picadas

Page 174
Jonathan Wallen

PLAY AND WORK AREAS
Page 177
Melanie Acevedo

Page 179
Paul Costello

Page 183
Pieter Estersohn

Page 185
Joshua McHugh

Page 186
Max Kim-Bee

Page 189
Pieter Estersohn

Page: 190
Costa Picadas

Page 191
Cindy Gold

Page 193
Melanie Acevedo

Page 194
Melanie Acevedo

Page 197
Thibault Jeanson

Pages 198 & 199
William Abranowicz

Page 200
Tria Giovan

Page 203
Thibault Jeanson

Page 204
Costa Picadas

Page 205
Costa Picadas

Pages 206 & 207
Tria Giovan

Page 208
Joshua McHugh

Page 209
Tim Street-Porter

Page 210
Paul Costello

Page 213
© William Abranowicz /
Art + Commerce

Page 214
© William Abranowicz /
Art + Commerce

Page 217
Tim Street-Porter

Page 218
Joshua McHugh

Page 220
Tria Giovan

Page 221
Michael Partenio

Page 222
John Gruen

Page 223
John Gruen

Page 225
Jean Randazzo

Page 226
Miguel Flores-Vianna

Page 227
Photographer of both
images: Costa Picadas

Page 228
Tria Giovan

Pages 230 & 231
Costa Picadas

Page 233
Joshua McHugh

Pages 234 & 235
Costa Picadas

Acknowledgments

Profuse thanks goes to the stellar group of interior designers, architects and photographers who so generously contributed to bringing this book to life. Its content wouldn't be half as glorious without their unique eyes and talents and I am indebted.

For my art director Deb Wood and the enthusiastic and endlessly supportive hands at Rizzoli: Charles Miers, Dung Ngo and especially my editor, Ellen Nidy, thank you!

First published in the United States of America in 2010 by
Rizzoli International Publications, Inc.
300 Park Avenue South, New York, NY 10010
www.rizzoliusa.com

© 2010 Rizzoli International Publishing, Inc.

© 2010 Susanna Salk

2010, 2011, 2012, 2013 / 10 9 8 7 6 5 4 3 2 1

ISBN-13: 978-0-8478-3416-7

Library of Congress Control Number: 2009940103

Printed in China

Distributed to the U.S trade by Random House